I0555026

The Glorious Mysteries

Scripture quotations are from New Revised Standard Version Bible: Catholic Edition, copyright © 1989, 1993 National Council of the Churches of Christ in the United States of America. Used by permission. All rights reserved worldwide.

The Glorious Mysteries
Copyright © 2023
Sara Swann

ISBN: 978-1-957344-91-1

Cover design by Mike Parker
Illustrations copyright © 2023 by Sara Swann. Used by permission, all rights reserved.

All rights reserved. No part of this book may be reproduced, stored in a retrieval system, or transmitted in any form or by any means—electronic, mechanical, photocopy, recording or otherwise—without the prior written permission of the publisher. The only exception is brief quotations for review purposes.

Published by WordCrafts Press
Cody, Wyoming 82414
www.wordcrafts.net

The Glorious Mysteries

Mysteries of the Rosary for Children
Volume 3

SARA SWANN

WordCrafts Press

To my third and glorious child, Dawson, the boy with the sweetest heart, best sense of humor, and kindest personality, not to mention a deep understanding of our Faith that impresses me to no end!
It is a blessing to watch you grow into the young man God intended you to be. Your mama is so proud of you.
I love you to the moon and back!

GETTING STARTED

The first step in praying your Rosary is to get ready. For each mystery below, the prayers you pray will be written in **bold**, so you know what to say, just like the responses you say in Mass, and their Latin translations are there in ***bold italics***, too.

Now, look at your Rosary. Every Rosary has a crucifix, a medallion, six big beads, and 53 smaller beads. All these beads help us pray lots of prayers, and that is just one of the many reasons that make the Rosary so special.

You might be asking, what prayers go where? There are only seven prayers you need to know to pray the Rosary.

1. The Sign of the Cross
2. The Apostles' Creed
3. The Hail Mary
4. The Glory Be
5. The Fatima Prayer
6. The Hail Holy Queen
7. The Final Prayer.

The Sign of the Cross always bookends, or begins and ends, the Rosary just as it begins and ends all our prayers.

The Crucifix is for the Apostle's Creed. The big beads are

for the Our Father prayer, and the small beads are for the Hail Mary. The other prayers are sprinkled throughout.

> **Did you know . . .**
> There is a very important difference between a cross and a Crucifix? A Crucifix is a cross with Jesus's body, called The Corpus, on it!

Are you ready to get started? Let's go!

WEDNESDAY AND SUNDAY

The Glorious Mysteries

During these Glorious Mysteries, you share in the experiences that Mother Mary and Jesus had beginning with the Jesus' Resurrection from death, all the way to Mary being assumed into Heaven. How glorious is that!

> **Did you know . . .**
> We pray these mysteries on Wednesdays and Sundays.

Begin with your Rosary in your hand.

Do the Sign of the Cross by touching your Rosary to your forehead, then your chest, then left shoulder, then your right shoulder.

You can remember this because God the Father is in Heaven above us (touch your forehead), God the Son lives in your heart (touch your chest), and Jesus carried the Cross on His shoulders (touch your left shoulder then your right shoulder). When you say amen, put your hands together in front of you, like prayer hands.

In the name of the Father,
> *In nomine Patris,*
>> *(Forehead)*

and of the Son,
> *et Filii,*
>> *(Chest or Heart)*

and of the Holy Spirit.
> *Et Spiritus Sancti.*
>> *(Left then Right Shoulder)*

Amen.
> *Amen.*
>> *(End with prayer hands)*

Now you are ready to begin praying your Rosary. First, hold the Crucifix and pray the Apostles' Creed.

I believe in God,
> *Credo in Deum*

the Father almighty,
> *Patrem omnipoténtem,*

Creator of heaven and earth,
> *Creatórem cæli et terræ.*

And in Jesus Christ,
> *Et in Iesum Christum,*

His only Son,
> *Fílium eius únicum,*

Our Lord,
> *Dóminum nostrum,*

Who was conceived by the Holy Spirit,
> *qui concéptus est de Spíritu Sancto,*

Born of the Virgin Mary,
> *natus ex María Vírgine,*

Suffered under Pontius Pilate,

passus sub Póntio Piláto,

Was crucified, died, and was buried;

crucifíxus, mórtuus, et sepúltus,

He descended into hell;

descéndit ad ínfernos,

On the third day;

tértia die;

He rose again from the dead;

resurréxit a mórtuis;

He ascended into Heaven,

ascéndit ad cælos,

And is seated at the right hand of God,

sedet ad déxteram Dei,

The Father Almighty,

Patris omnipoténtis,

And from there He will come

inde ventúrus

to judge the living and the dead.

est iudicáre vivos et mórtuos.

I believe in the Holy Spirit,

Credo in Spíritum Sanctum,

The Holy Catholic Church,

sanctam Ecclésiam cathólicam,

The communion of Saints,

sanctórum communiónem,

The forgiveness of sins,

remissiónem peccatórum,

The resurrection of the body,

carnis resurrectiónem,

And life everlasting.

vitam ætérnam.

Amen.

Amen.

Now, move your fingers up to the next bead. It is bigger than the other beads and may even be a different color, so you know this bead is for the Our Father prayer.

Our Father, who art in heaven,

Pater noster, qui es in cælis,

hallowed be Thy name.

sanctificétur nomen tuum.

Thy kingdom come,

Advéniat regnum tuum.

Thy will be done,

Fiat volúntas tua,

On earth as it is in heaven.

sicut in cælo, et in terra.

And give us this day our daily bread,

Panem nostrum quotidiánum da nobis hódie,

And forgive us our trespasses,

et dimítte nobis débita nostra sicut

As we forgive those who trespass against us,

et nos dimíttimus debitóribus nostris.

And lead us not into temptation,

Et ne nos indúcas in tentatiónem,

But deliver us from evil.

sed líbera nos a malo.

Amen.

Amen.

Did you know . . .
Charity is love.

Next, we have three small beads. You already know these are for the Hail Mary prayers. Each one of these three beads are special for a different reason. These special beads help open our hearts to be more like Mother Mary in our own *Faith*, *Hope*, and *Charity*.

Move your fingers to the first Hail Mary bead. This Hail Mary bead is the *Faith* bead. We ask for an increase in our Faith as we pray the Hail Mary prayer.

Hail Mary, full of grace,
> *Ave María, grátia plena,*

the Lord is with thee.
> *Dóminus tecum.*

Blessed art thou amongst women,
> *Benedícta tu in muliéribus,*

and blessed is the fruit of thy womb, Jesus.
> *et benedíctus fructus ventris tui, Iesus.*

Holy Mary, Mother of God,
> *Sancta María, Mater Dei,*

Pray for us sinners,
> *ora pro nobis peccatóribus,*

Now and at the hour of our death.
> *nunc, et in hora mortis nostræ.*

Amen.
> *Amen.*

Now, move your fingers to the second small bead. On this bead, we pray the Hail Mary prayer and ask for an increase in our *Hope*.

Hail Mary, full of grace,
> *Ave María, grátia plena,*

the Lord is with thee.
> *Dóminus tecum.*

Blessed art thou amongst women,
> *Benedícta tu in muliéribus,*

and blessed is the fruit of thy womb, Jesus.

et benedíctus fructus ventris tui,Iesus.

Holy Mary, Mother of God,

Sancta María, Mater Dei,

Pray for us sinners,

ora pro nobis peccatóribus,

Now and at the hour of our death.

nunc, et in hora mortis nostræ.

Amen.

Amen.

Finally, move your fingers to the third small bead. On this bead, we pray the Hail Mary prayer and ask for an increase in our *Charity*.

Hail Mary, full of grace,

Ave María, grátia plena,

the Lord is with thee.

Dóminus tecum.

Blessed art thou amongst women,

Benedícta tu in muliéribus,

and blessed is the fruit of thy womb, Jesus.

et benedíctus fructus ventris tui, Iesus.

Holy Mary, Mother of God,

Sancta María, Mater Dei,

Pray for us sinners,

ora pro nobis peccatóribus,

Now and at the hour of our death.

nunc, et in hora mortis nostræ.

Amen.

Amen.

Remember those surprise prayers we talked about earlier? Here is the first time you find them in the Rosary! With your fingers still on the bead, you say two very special prayers.

First, is the Glory Be.

When you say the Glory Be prayer, you bow to the Crucifix to show respect and love to Jesus Christ.

Then, you say the Fatima Prayer. Sometimes, the Fatima Prayer is sometimes called the O My Jesus prayer.

Glory Be

Glória

to the Father,

Patri,

and to the Son,

et Fílio,

and to the Holy Spirit.

et Spirítui Sancto.

As it was in the beginning,

Sicut erat in princípio,

Is now,

et nunc,

And ever shall be,

et semper,

World without end.

et in sæcula sæculórum.

Amen.

Amen.

Did you remember . . .
to bow to your crucifix whenever
you pray a Glory Be?

Then, pray your Fatima Prayer.

O My Jesus,

Dómine Jesu,

Forgive us our sins,

dimitte nobis débita nostra,

And save us from the fires of hell.

salva nos ab igne inferni,

Lead all souls to heaven,

perduc in caelum omnes ánimas,

Especially those in most need of thy

praesertim eas, quae misericórdiae tuae

mercy.

máxime indigent.

Now you're ready to begin your first Glorius Mystery!

The First Glorious Mystery

The Resurrection

The First Glorious Mystery comes from the Gospel of St. Luke. The Scripture for the first Glorious Mystery tells us why this mystery is important..

But on the first day of the week, at early dawn, they went to the tomb, taking the spices which they had prepared.

And they found the stone rolled away from the tomb, but when they went in they did not find the body.

While they were perplexed about this, behold, two men stood by them in dazzling apparel; and as they were frightened and bowed their faces to the ground, the men said to them, 'Why do you seek the living among the dead? He is not here, but has risen'.

St. Luke 24:1–5

Thoughts to Consider . . .
The fruit of this mystery is faith.

Move up to the next big bead. Remember, this is an Our Father bead.

Our Father, who art in heaven,
> *Pater noster, qui es in cælis,*

hallowed be Thy name.
> *sanctificétur nomen tuum.*

Thy kingdom come,
> *Advéniat regnum tuum.*

Thy will be done,
> *Fiat volúntas tua,*

On earth as it is in heaven.
> *sicut in cælo, et in terra.*

And give us this day our daily bread,
> *Panem nostrum quotidiánum da nobis hódie,*

And forgive us our trespasses,
> *et dimítte nobis débita nostra sicut*

As we forgive those who trespass against us,
> *et nos dimíttimus debitóribus nostris.*

And lead us not into temptation,
> *Et ne nos indúcas in tentatiónem,*

But deliver us from evil.
> *sed líbera nos a malo.*

Amen.
> *Amen.*

> **Pro Tip . . .**
> Move to the next bead each time you
> say *amen.*

Next, pray ten Hail Mary prayers while you think about the Scripture. We also think about how we can be more modest and humble.

Hail Mary, full of grace,
> *Ave María, grátia plena,*

the Lord is with thee.
> *Dóminus tecum.*

Blessed art thou amongst women,
> *Benedícta tu in muliéribus,*

and blessed is the fruit of thy womb, Jesus.
> *et benedíctus fructus ventris tui, Iesus.*

Holy Mary, Mother of God,
> *Sancta María, Mater Dei,*

Pray for us sinners,
> *ora pro nobis peccatóribus,*

Now and at the hour of our death.
> *nunc, et in hora mortis nostræ.*

Amen.
> *Amen.*

Remember the two special prayers, The Glory Be and The Fatima Prayer, that are hidden throughout our Rosary? You just found them again! Keep holding the tenth bead and pray a Glory Be and a Fatima Prayer. Remember to bow to your Crucifix when you pray your Glory Be.

Glory Be

Glória

to the Father,

Patri,

and to the Son,

et Fílio,

and to the Holy Spirit.

et Spirítui Sancto.

As it was in the beginning,

Sicut erat in princípio,

Is now,

et nunc,

And ever shall be,

et semper,

World without end.

et in sæcula sæculórum.

Amen.

Amen.

Did you know . . .
Many people saw Jesus after the Resurrection.

Then, pray your Fatima Prayer.

O My Jesus,

Dómine Jesu,

Forgive us our sins,

> *dimitte nobis débita nostra,*

And save us from the fires of hell.

> *salva nos ab igne inferni,*

Lead all souls to heaven,

> *perduc in caelum omnes ánimas,*

Especially those in most need of thy

> *praesertim eas, quae misericórdiae tuae*

mercy.

> *máxime indigent.*

Did you know . . .

The Rosary is divided into sets of ten Hail Mary prayers called decades. There are five decades in one full Rosary

---

Congratulations! You have just finished praying your first decade of the Rosary! As you prayed, you thought about how you can keep the faith in your own life, just like the early Christians. What are some ways you can keep faith in your life, just like the early Christians? Write down some of your thoughts on the next page.

The Second Glorious Mystery

The Ascension

*T*he Second Joyful Mystery comes from the Gospel of St. Mark and tells us why this mystery is important.

So then the Lord Jesus, after he had spoken to them, was taken up into heaven, and sat down at the right hand of God.

St. Mark 16:19

Thoughts to Consider . . .

The fruit of this mystery is hope for Heaven. How can you shape your life on earth so that you get to live in Heaven with Jesus for all eternity?

Move your fingers to the next big, Our Father bead.

Our Father, who art in heaven,
Pater noster, qui es in cælis,
hallowed be Thy name.
sanctificétur nomen tuum.
Thy kingdom come,
Advéniat regnum tuum.
Thy will be done,
Fiat volúntas tua,
On earth as it is in heaven.
sicut in cælo, et in terra.
And give us this day our daily bread,
Panem nostrum quotidiánum da nobis hódie,
And forgive us our trespasses,
et dimítte nobis débita nostra sicut
As we forgive those who trespass against us,
et nos dimíttimus debitóribus nostris.

And lead us not into temptation,

> *Et ne nos indúcas in tentatiónem,*

But deliver us from evil.

> *sed líbera nos a malo.*

Amen.

> *Amen.*

Move your fingers along the beads as you pray ten Hail Mary prayers and think about the Scripture. Also think about ways you can shape your life in a way that focuses on spending eternity in Heaven with Jesus.

Hail Mary, full of grace,

> *Ave María, grátia plena,*

the Lord is with thee.

> *Dóminus tecum.*

Blessed art thou amongst women,

> *Benedícta tu in muliéribus,*

and blessed is the fruit of thy womb, Jesus.

> *et benedíctus fructus ventris tui, Iesus.*

Holy Mary, Mother of God,

> *Sancta María, Mater Dei,*

Pray for us sinners,

> *ora pro nobis peccatóribus,*

Now and at the hour of our death.

> *nunc, et in hora mortis nostræ.*

Amen.

> *Amen.*

Did you know . . .

When you pray the Rosary, you are offering Mother Mary a bouquet of roses in Heaven! That is why it is called a Rosary.

Keep holding the tenth bead and pray a Glory Be and a Fatima Prayer. Remember to bow to your crucifix when you pray your Glory Be.

Glory Be

Glória

to the Father,

Patri,

and to the Son,

et Fílio,

and to the Holy Spirit.

et Spirítui Sancto.

As it was in the beginning,

Sicut erat in princípio,

Is now,

et nunc,

And ever shall be,

et semper,

World without end.

et in sæcula sæculórum.

Amen.

Amen.

Then, pray your Fatima Prayer.

O My Jesus,

Dómine Jesu,

Forgive us our sins,

dimitte nobis débita nostra,

And save us from the fires of hell.

salva nos ab igne inferni,

Lead all souls to heaven,

perduc in caelum omnes ánimas,

Especially those in most need of thy

praesertim eas, quae misericórdiae tuae

mercy.

máxime indigent.

Did you know . . .

All the mysteries of the Rosary are taken from Scripture.

How about that! You have just finished praying your second decade of the Glorious Mysteries of Rosary!

As you prayed, you thought about how you can hope for Heaven in your life and by your actions. What are some ways you can show the world that you look forward to spending eternity with Jesus? Write down some of your ideas of how to do this on the next page.

The Third Glorious Mystery

The Descent of the Holy Spirit

The Third Glorious Mystery comes from the Book of Acts and tells us the story of Pentecost.

When the day of Pentecost had come, they were all together in one place.

And suddenly a sound came from heaven like the rush of a mighty wind, and it filled all the house where they were sitting.

And there appeared to them tongues as of fire, distributed and resting on each one of them.

And they were all filled with the Holy Spirit and began to speak in other tongues, as the Spirit gave them utterance.

Acts 2:1–4

Thoughts to Consider . . .

The fruits of this mystery are wisdom and the love of God. How can you show your fearless love for God, like the Apostles did?

Move your fingers to the next big, Our Father bead.

Our Father, who art in heaven,

Pater noster, qui es in cælis,

hallowed be Thy name.

sanctificétur nomen tuum.

Thy kingdom come,

Advéniat regnum tuum.

Thy will be done,

Fiat volúntas tua,

On earth as it is in heaven.

sicut in cælo, et in terra.

And give us this day our daily bread,

Panem nostrum quotidiánum da nobis hódie,

And forgive us our trespasses,

> *dimítte nobis débita nostra sicut*

As we forgive those who trespass against us,

> *et nos dimíttimus debitóribus nostris.*

And lead us not into temptation,

> *Et ne nos indúcas in tentatiónem,*

But deliver us from evil.

> *sed líbera nos a malo.*

Amen.

> *Amen.*

Move your fingers along the beads as you pray ten Hail Mary prayers and think about the Scripture. Also think about ways you can be fearless in your love for God.

Hail Mary, full of grace,

> *Ave María, grátia plena,*

the Lord is with thee.

> *Dóminus tecum.*

Blessed art thou amongst women,

> *Benedícta tu in muliéribus,*

and blessed is the fruit of thy womb, Jesus.

> *et benedíctus fructus ventris tui, Iesus.*

Holy Mary, Mother of God,

> *Sancta María, Mater Dei,*

Pray for us sinners,

> *ora pro nobis peccatóribus,*

Now and at the hour of our death.

> *nunc, et in hora mortis nostræ.*

Amen.

> *Amen.*

Keep holding the tenth bead and pray a Glory Be and a Fatima

Prayer. Remember to bow to your crucifix when you pray your
Glory Be.

Glory Be

Glória

to the Father,

Patri,

and to the Son,

et Fílio,

and to the Holy Spirit.

et Spirítui Sancto.

As it was in the beginning,

Sicut erat in princípio,

Is now,

et nunc,

And ever shall be,

et semper,

World without end.

et in sæcula sæculórum.

Amen.

Amen.

> ### Did you know . . .
> Did you know that St. Padre Pio calls the
> Rosary a weapon? At the Battle of Lepanto
> on October 7, 1571, the Christians laid down
> their weapons and all prayed the Rosary at
> the urging of the Pope.

Now, it's time for the Fatima Prayer.

O My Jesus,

Dómine Jesu,

Forgive us our sins,
> *dimitte nobis débita nostra,*

And save us from the fires of hell.
> *salva nos ab igne inferni.*

Lead all souls to heaven,
> *perduc in caelum omnes ánimas,*

Especially those in most need of thy
> *praesertim eas, quae misericórdiae tuae*

mercy.
> *máxime indigent.*

Great job! You have just finished praying your third decade the Glorious Mysteries of Rosary!

Did you know . . .

As a result of praying the Rosary all together, the Christians celebrated an overwhelming victory over the Ottoman Empire, and they credited Mother Mary with the victory. They even honored her with a new title, Our Lady of Victory.

As you prayed, you thought about how you can live fearlessly for God. What are some ways you can live fearlessly for God like the early Apostles did, as well as those Christians who prayed the Rosary during the Battle of Lepanto? On the next page, write down some of your ideas of how you can live fearlessly.

The Fourth Glorious Mystery

The Assumption of Mary into Heaven

Τhe Fourth Glorious Mystery comes from the Gospel of St. Luke.

Henceforth all generations will call me blessed; for he who is mighty has done great things for me.
                                                    St. Luke 1:48–49

Thoughts to Consider . . .
The fruit of this mystery is devotion to Mother Mary.

Move your fingers to the next big, Our Father bead.

Our Father, who art in heaven,
                    Pater noster, qui es in cælis,
hallowed be Thy name.
                    sanctificétur nomen tuum.
Thy kingdom come,
                    Advéniat regnum tuum.
Thy will be done,
                    Fiat volúntas tua,
On earth as it is in heaven.
                    sicut in cælo, et in terra.
And give us this day our daily bread,
                Panem nostrum quotidiánum da nobis hódie,
And forgive us our trespasses,
                    et dimítte nobis débita nostra sicut
As we forgive those who trespass against us,
                    et nos dimíttimus debitóribus nostris.
And lead us not into temptation,
                    Et ne nos indúcas in tentatiónem,
But deliver us from evil.
                    sed líbera nos a malo.
Amen.
                    Amen.

Move your fingers along the beads as you pray ten Hail Mary prayers and think about the Scripture. Also think about ways you can show your devotion to Jesus's mother in your life.

Hail Mary, full of grace,

> *Ave María, grátia plena,*

the Lord is with thee.

> *Dóminus tecum.*

Blessed art thou amongst women,

> *Benedícta tu in muliéribus,*

and blessed is the fruit of thy womb, Jesus.

> *et benedíctus fructus ventris tui, Iesus.*

Holy Mary, Mother of God,

> *Sancta María, Mater Dei,*

Pray for us sinners,

> *ora pro nobis peccatóribus,*

Now and at the hour of our death.

> *nunc, et in hora mortis nostræ.*

Amen.

> *Amen.*

Keep holding the tenth bead and pray a Glory Be and a Fatima Prayer. Remember to bow to your crucifix when you pray your Glory Be.

Thoughts to Consider . . .

St. Maximillian Kolbe, a Saint who gave his life for another man at Auschwitz Concentration Camp, said: "Never be afraid of loving the Blessed Mother too much. You can never love her more than Jesus did."

Glory Be

Glória

to the Father,

Patri,

and to the Son,

et Fílio,

and to the Holy Spirit.

et Spirítui Sancto.

As it was in the beginning,

Sicut erat in princípio,

Is now,

et nunc,

And ever shall be,

et semper,

World without end.

et in sæcula sæculórum.

Amen.

Amen.

Now, it's time for the Fatima Prayer.

O My Jesus,

Dómine Jesu,

Forgive us our sins,

dimitte nobis débita nostra,

And save us from the fires of hell.

salva nos ab igne inferni,

Lead all souls to heaven,

perduc in caelum omnes ánimas,

Especially those in most need of thy

praesertim eas, quae misericórdiae tuae

mercy.

máxime indigent.

Look how far you've come! You have just finished praying your fourth decade of the Rosary!

As you prayed, you thought about how you can show Mother Mary how much you love her. Can you think of some ways you can show Mother Mary and your own mother how much you love them? Write down some of your ideas about how to express your love for them on the next page.

_____

_____

_____

_____

_____

_____

_____

_____

_____

_____

_____

_____

_____

_____

_____

_____

_____

_____

_____

_____

_____

_____

_____

_____

_____

_____

_____

_____

_____

_____

The Fifth Glorious Mystery

The Coronation of Mary as The Queen of Heaven

The Fifth Glorious Mystery comes from the Book of Revelation.

And a great portent appeared in Heaven, a woman clothed with the sun, with the moon under her feet, and on her head a crown of twelve stars.

Revelations 12:1

Thoughts to Consider . . .
The fruit of this mystery is eternal life.

Move your fingers to the next big, Our Father bead.

Our Father, who art in heaven,
> *Pater noster, qui es in cælis,*

hallowed be Thy name.
> *sanctificétur nomen tuum.*

Thy kingdom come,
> *Advéniat regnum tuum.*

Thy will be done,
> *Fiat volúntas tua,*

On earth as it is in heaven.
> *sicut in cælo, et in terra.*

And give us this day our daily bread,
> *Panem nostrum quotidiánum da nobis hódie,*

And forgive us our trespasses,
> *et dimítte nobis débita nostra sicut*

As we forgive those who trespass against us,
> *et nos dimíttimus debitóribus nostris.*

And lead us not into temptation,
> *Et ne nos indúcas in tentatiónem,*

But deliver us from evil.

sed líbera nos a malo.

Amen.

Amen.

Move your fingers along the beads as you pray ten Hail Mary prayers and think about the Scripture. Think about how wonderful it was when Mother Mary was crowned Queen of Heaven for all eternity!

> **Did you know . . .**
> A coronation means a crowning.

Hail Mary, full of grace,

Ave María, grátia plena,

the Lord is with thee.

Dóminus tecum.

Blessed art thou amongst women,

Benedícta tu in muliéribus,

and blessed is the fruit of thy womb, Jesus.

et benedíctus fructus ventris tui, Iesus.

Holy Mary, Mother of God,

Sancta María, Mater Dei,

Pray for us sinners,

ora pro nobis peccatóribus,

Now and at the hour of our death.

nunc, et in hora mortis nostræ.

Amen.

Amen.

Keep holding the tenth bead and pray a Glory Be and a Fatima Prayer. Remember to bow to your crucifix when you pray your Glory Be.

Glory Be

Glória

to the Father,

Patri,

and to the Son,

et Fílio,

and to the Holy Spirit.

et Spirítui Sancto.

As it was in the beginning,

Sicut erat in princípio,

Is now,

et nunc,

And ever shall be,

et semper,

World without end.

et in sæcula sæculórum.

Amen.

Amen.

Now, it's time for the Fatima Prayer.

O My Jesus,

Dómine Jesu,

Forgive us our sins,

dimitte nobis débita nostra,

And save us from the fires of hell.

salva nos ab igne inferni,

Lead all souls to heaven,

perduc in caelum omnes ánimas,

Especially those in most need of thy

praesertim eas, quae misericórdiae tuae

mercy.

máxime indigent.

You're almost finished praying your entire decade of the Glorious Mysteries of the Rosary!

Thoughts to Consider . . .

In the Sorrowful mysteries, we know Mother Mary was sad when her Son was crucified. Imagine how happy she is to spend all of eternity at his side in Heaven!

As you prayed, you thought about Mother Mary being crowned Queen of Heaven for all eternity. Do you have faith that you will spend eternity with Jesus and His Blessed Mother? Write down some of your ideas about eternal happiness with Jesus and His Blessed Mother on the next page.

The Mystery of the Rosary

The Ending of Each Mystery

The ending of each Mystery of the Rosary consists of two very special prayers: The Hail Holy Queen and The Final Prayer.

Hail Holy Queen

Hail Holy Queen,

> *Salve Regína,*

Mother of Mercy,

> *mater misericórdiæ;*

our Life, our Sweetness, and our hope.

> *vita, dulcédo, et spes nostra, salve.*

To thee we cry,

> *Ad te Clamámus*

poor banished children of Eve.

> *éxsules fílii Evæ;*

To thee we send up our sighs,

> *Ad te Suspirámus,*

mourning and weeping in this valley of tears.

> *geméntes et flentes in hac lacrimárum valle.*

41

Turn then most gracious advocate,

Eia ergo, Advocáta nostra,

Thine eyes of mercy toward us,

Illos tuos misericórdes óculos ad nos convérte:

and after this, our exile,

Et Iesum, benedíctum fructum

show unto us,

ventris tui, Nobis post hoc exsílium

the blessed fruit of thy womb, Jesus.

osténde.

O clement, O loving, O sweet Virgin Mary.

O clemens, o pia, o dulcis Virgo María.

Pray for us O Holy Mother of God,

Ora pro nobis, Sancta Dei Genetrix.

that we may be made worthy

Ut digni efficiamur

of the promises of Christ.

promissiónibus Christi.

Amen.

Amen.

The Final Prayer ends each Mystery of the Rosary.

Let us pray.

Oremus.

O God, whose only begotten Son,

Déus, cújus Unigénitus

by His life, death, and resurrection,

per vítam, mortem, et resurrectiónem

has purchased for us the

Súam nóbis salútis

rewards of eternal life,

ætérnæ præmia comparávit:

grant, we beseech Thee,

concéde, quǽsumus:

that meditating upon these mysteries

ut hæc mystéria

of the Most Holy Rosary of

sacratíssimo beátæ

the Blessed Virgin Mary,

Maríæ Vírginis Rosário recoléntes,

we may imitate what they contain

et imitémur quod cóntinent,

and obtain what they promise,

et quod promíttunt, assequámur.

through the same Christ Our Lord.

Per eúndem Chrístum Dóminum nóstrum.

Amen.

Amen.

Remember what bookends all your prayers—including your Rosary prayers—The Sign of the Cross.

In the name of the Father,

In nomine Patris,

(Forehead)

and of the Son,

et Filii,

(Chest or Heart)

and of the Holy Spirit.

Et Spiritus Sancti.

(Left then Right Shoulder)

Amen.

Amen.

(End with prayer hands)

Acknowledgements

There are so many I would like to thank for helping the Mysteries of the Rosary for Children series come to fruition. My children, who not only stood by me as I taught myself to draw and then to paint in order to create the illustrations for this series, but drew and painted right along with me. My parents, who not only encouraged this project from the beginning, but were just as excited as me as each painting progressed and came to *life*. To my publishers, Mike and Paula, as they championed this project from the beginning, deep within the throes of the pandemic.

And the angel said to them: Fear not; for, behold, I bring you good tidings of great joy that shall be to all the people. For today, a Savior has been born for you in the city of David: he is Christ the Lord. And this will be a sign for you: you will find the infant wrapped in swaddling clothes and lying in a manger. And suddenly there was with the Angel a multitude of the celestial army, praising God and saying, Glory to God in the highest, and on earth peace to men of good will.

St. Luke 2:10–14 NIV

Sara Swann-Barnard BSN, RN

About the Author

Sara Swann loves to write and has more than thirty credited works available in print.

She holds a Bachelor of Arts degree in History and spent several years as a teacher in West Texas before earning a Bachelor of Science degree in Nursing. She now works as an emergency room nurse in Houston, Texas, where she, her children, and their menagerie of rescue pets—six in all—make their home.

In her spare time, Sara and her family enjoy ice cream and the beach, but she wishes someone who majored in Physics and Engineering would hurry up and invent a time machine so she could meet St. Francis of Assisi, Henry VIII, William Wallace, and Vlad the Impaler.

Connect with Sara online at:

www.NurseSaraBooks.com

ALSO AVAILABLE FROM

WordCrafts Press

In The Boat with Jesus
by Marian Rizzo

Illuminations
by Paula K. Parker

Finding God in the Bathroom
by Rev. Brian C. Johnson, PhD

Donkey Tales
by Keith Alexis

www.wordcrafts.net.

www.ingramcontent.com/pod-product-compliance
Lightning Source LLC
Chambersburg PA
CBHW070945120626
46546CB00004B/1574